THIS IS AN UNOFFICIAL, UNAUTHORIZED, AND INDEPENDENT PARODY BOOK.

PUBLISHED IN 2015 BY
RAZZBERRY BOOKS
EMAIL: INFO@RAZZBERRYBOOKS.COM

PRINTED IN THE UNITED STATES OF AMERICA

ISBN-13: 978-0692435878

I0087298

JON HAMM COLORING BOOK

RUN TO JON HAMM.
RUN TO HIM.

www.ingramcontent.com/pod-product-compliance
Lightning Source LLC
Chambersburg PA
CBHW081229040426
42445CB00016B/1922